TEAM SPIRIT®

SMART BOOKS FOR YOUNG FANS

THE DALLAS COWBOYS

BY

MARK STEWART

New Hanover County Public Library
201 Chestnut Street
Wilmington, North Carolina 28401

NORWOOD HOUSE PRESS

CHICAGO, ILLINOIS

Norwood House Press
P.O. Box 316598
Chicago, Illinois 60631

For information regarding Norwood House Press, please visit our website at:
www.norwoodhousepress.com or call 866-565-2900.

All photos courtesy of Getty Images except the following:
Icon SMI (4, 12), Topps, Inc. (6, 15, 30, 34 right, 43 top),
Black Book Partners (10, 11, 14, 35 top right, 36, 37, 38, 39, 40, 41, 42 bottom left, 43 bottom),
Philadelphia Gum Company (20, 42 top left), Ideal Publishing Corp. (26), Dallas Cowboys/NFL (27, 33, 45),
Author's Collection (42 bottom), Matt Richman (48).
Cover Photo: Icon SMI

The memorabilia and artifacts pictured in this book are presented for educational and informational purposes,
and come from the collection of the author.

Editor: Mike Kennedy
Designer: Ron Jaffe
Project Management: Black Book Partners, LLC.
Special thanks to Topps, Inc.

Library of Congress Cataloging-in-Publication Data

Stewart, Mark, 1960-
    The Dallas Cowboys / by Mark Stewart. -- Rev. ed.
      p. cm. -- (Team spirit)
    Includes bibliographical references and index.
    Summary: "A revised Team Spirit Football edition featuring the Dallas
Cowboys that chronicles the history and accomplishments of the team.
Includes access to the Team Spirit website which provides additional
information and photos"--Provided by publisher.
    ISBN 978-1-59953-520-3 (library edition : alk. paper) -- ISBN
978-1-60357-462-4 (ebook)
    1. Dallas Cowboys (Football team)--Juvenile literature. I. Title.
    GV956.D3S745 2012
    796.332'64097642821--dc23
                                                2012016656

Manufactured in the United States of America in North Mankato, Minnesota.
237R—082013

COVER PHOTO: The Cowboys celebrate a touchdown during the 2011 season.

Table of Contents

ABOUT OUR GLOSSARY

In this book, there may be several words that you are reading for the first time. Some are sports words, some are new vocabulary words, and some are familiar words that are used in an unusual way. All of these words are defined on page 46. Throughout the book, sports words appear in **bold type**. Regular vocabulary words appear in *bold italic type*.

The greatness of a sports team can be measured in many ways. Championships are one way to do it. Or, you can count the number of superstars who have played for the team. You can also look at how many fans root for those superstars and their teammates. By any of these measures, the Dallas Cowboys are one of the most remarkable teams in sports.

The Cowboys take winning seriously. They may be fun-loving off the field, but on the field every player and coach is focused on achieving victory. This *tradition* started more than 50 years ago. It is stronger than ever today.

This book tells the story of the Cowboys. They have been called "America's Team" because they have fans all over the country. However, when the day is done, the Cowboys aren't playing for America. They are playing for pride—and to win championships.

Jay Ratliff and DeMarcus Ware celebrate a game-changing play.

ootball fans in Texas had a lot to talk about when the 1960 season began. One year earlier, there were no **professional** teams in the state. Suddenly there were three. The **National Football League (NFL)** was expanding and placed a team in Dallas called the Cowboys. The **American Football League (AFL)** did the same and put a team in Dallas called the Texans. The AFL also started a team in Houston called the Oilers.

A businessman named Clint Murchison owned the Cowboys. He had made millions of dollars in the oil industry. Murchison originally had a deal to buy the Washington Redskins, but it fell through. That began a long **rivalry** between the Cowboys and Redskins. In 1960, however, Murchison and his team had other things to worry about. The Cowboys did not win a single game in their first year. Meanwhile, the Texans had a

BOB LILLY
DALLAS COWBOYS
DEFENSIVE TACKLE

winning record, and the Oilers took the AFL championship!

The Cowboys still had an advantage. Their fans were crazy about the team and filled the stadium for every game. The Texans got the message and moved to Kansas City, where they became the Chiefs.

The Cowboys had one of football's most brilliant coaches, Tom Landry. He got plenty of help from Gil Brandt and Tex Schramm, who ran the team's business off the field. Together, these three built Dallas into a winner by the end of the 1960s. The Cowboys had loads of talent during this time. Their stars on offense included Don Meredith, Craig Morton, Don Perkins, Dan Reeves, Bob Hayes, and Ralph Neely. The defense was led by Bob Lilly, Jethro Pugh, Chuck Howley, Lee Roy Jordan, and Mel Renfro. They helped Dallas reach the **NFL Championship Game** in 1966 and again in 1967.

Cowboys fans had to wait until the 1970s before they got to watch their team play in the **Super Bowl**. Dallas advanced to the big game five times during the *decade* and won the championship twice.

LEFT: Bob Lilly   **ABOVE**: Tom Landry poses with quarterbacks Roger Staubach and Craig Morton.

Landry was still the coach, but a new group of players now led the team. Roger Staubach, Calvin Hill, Drew Pearson, Rayfield Wright, and Tony Dorsett were the stars on offense. Harvey Martin, Randy White, Ed "Too Tall" Jones, Cliff Harris, and Charlie Waters led a hard-hitting defense.

Eventually, the Cowboys had to rebuild their club. Normally, this takes many years, but Dallas did it much faster. The Cowboys traded star running back Herschel Walker for a group of talented young players. In 1989, the Cowboys hired an excellent coach in Jimmy Johnson and also made three brilliant picks in the **draft**: Troy Aikman, Michael Irvin, and Emmitt Smith. This trio continued the team's winning tradition. They got plenty of help from players such as Jay Novacek, Daryl Johnston, Erik Williams, Nate Newton, Charles Haley, Darren Woodson, Ken Norton Jr., and Russell Maryland. Dallas added other exciting stars, including

LEFT: Emmitt Smith slips through the arms of a tackler.
ABOVE: Touchdown! Michael Irvin reached the end zone 65 times during his career.

Deion Sanders and Rocket Ismail. The Cowboys returned to the Super Bowl three times during the 1990s—and won it every time.

As the 21st century began, the team had to rebuild again. This time the process was slower than in the past. The Cowboys did not have Landry or Johnson to rely on. Team owner Jerry Jones took on much of the responsibility of reshaping the Cowboys. Unfortunately, Dallas fell on hard times and had three losing seasons in a row from 2000 to 2002.

Slowly but surely, the team showed signs of improvement. Tony Romo developed into a **Pro Bowl** quarterback. Marion Barber and Julius Jones gave the Cowboys a good one-two punch in the running game. Jason Witten became one of the NFL's best tight ends.

The Cowboys also added top players to their defense. No one was better than DeMarcus Ware. He was a powerful linebacker with tremendous speed. He became known as the best pass-rusher in team history.

In 2007, the Cowboys looked like they were ready to return to the Super Bowl. They had the best record in the **National Football Conference (NFC)** during the regular season. However, Dallas suffered a disappointing loss in the **playoffs**. Two years later, Jerry Jones gave Cowboys fans something big to cheer about. The team opened a magnificent new stadium that held more than 80,000 people. Going to games in Dallas had always been a major event. Now it was like walking into a palace.

The Cowboys continue to build on their past success. They do their best to live up to the team's long tradition of winning. The Cowboys and their fans begin each season expecting to win—and knowing they have a great chance to be champions again.

LEFT: Jason Witten
ABOVE: DeMarcus Ware

Home Turf

The first home of the Cowboys was the Cotton Bowl in Dallas. In 1971, the team moved to Texas Stadium. It was located in the city of Irving, just a few minutes outside Dallas. The roof in Texas Stadium had a large oval opening right above the playing field. Fans joked that it allowed God to watch his favorite team play.

In 2009, the Cowboys opened a new stadium that was built with the fans in mind. It is the largest domed stadium in the world and also has a *retractable* roof, which can open or close depending on the weather. The stadium includes the team's *Hall of Fame* and two enormous video screens that hang above the field.

BY THE NUMBERS

- The Cowboys' stadium has 80,000 seats and can expand to more than 100,000 seats.
- In 2009, the Cowboys set an NFL record for attendance with 105,121 fans for a game against the New York Giants.
- Two arches run the length of the stadium. Each stands 300 feet tall.

The Cowboys know how to get their fans fired up!

Dressed for Success

There is no mistaking the Dallas *logo*. It's a big blue Star of Texas. The team has used this logo since its first season. It appears on both sides of the Cowboys' silver helmet.

Blue and silver are the main colors of the Dallas uniform. The team has worn the same basic style since the mid-1960s. Before that, the Cowboys' uniform was blue and white with stars on the shoulders. The team wears this "throwback" style for special games.

The Cowboys believe that their white uniforms are lucky. They wear them whenever possible, including home games. Sometimes, an opponent will put on white jerseys to force the Cowboys to play in blue.

Mel
RENFRO
DALLAS COWBOYS • DEF. BACK

LEFT: Tony Romo wears a "throwback" uniform made to look like the one the team wore in the early 1960s. **ABOVE**: Mel Renfro models the team's 1968 uniform.

We Won!

The Cowboys have a proud tradition of playing championship football. In their first 50 years, they won five Super Bowls. Only the Pittsburgh Steelers have won more. The Cowboys played in a total of eight Super Bowls during this time. The Steelers tied this record in 2008.

The team's first championship came in 1971, in Super Bowl VI. The Cowboys beat the Miami Dolphins, 24–3. The Dallas defense was tough all day. Chuck Howley intercepted a pass and recovered a **fumble**. Meanwhile, the Dallas offense rolled to 252 rushing yards. Quarterback Roger Staubach threw two touchdown passes and was named **Most Valuable Player (MVP)**. After the game, he said that the entire defense deserved the award.

The Cowboys won their next championship six years later over the Denver Broncos in Super Bowl XII. Staubach was still

LEFT: The Cowboys gave the Baltimore Colts no room to move during Super Bowl V.
RIGHT: Tom Landry gets a victory ride after Super Bowl XII.

the leader on offense, but the defense featured several new stars, including Randy White and Harvey Martin. The Cowboys took an early lead on a touchdown run by Tony Dorsett. They were up 13–0 at halftime.

The Broncos came alive in the third quarter and tried to make the game close. But the Cowboys responded with two scoring passes. The first was a 45-yard bomb from Staubach to Butch Johnson. The second was a trick play. Running back Robert Newhouse fooled the Denver defense and lofted a scoring toss to Golden Richards. The defense took over from there. White and Martin shared the MVP award.

It was more than a decade before the Cowboys celebrated their next championship. By then, Dallas had rebuilt around quarterback Troy Aikman, running back Emmitt Smith, and receiver Michael Irvin. They were the heart of an offense that could *dominate* with the run or the pass.

The Cowboys faced the Buffalo Bills in Super Bowl XXVII. The Bills never knew what hit them. Dallas scored four touchdowns in the first half, three on passes from Aikman. The second half wasn't much different. Aikman threw for his fourth touchdown of the day,

and Smith ran all over the Buffalo defense. The Cowboys cruised to a 52–17 victory. Aikman was the easy choice as the game's MVP.

The Cowboys played the Bills in a rematch a year later in Super Bowl XXVIII. This time Buffalo was ready. The Bills took a 13–6 lead into halftime, but the second half was all Dallas. In the third quarter, Leon Lett caused a fumble, and James Washington scooped it up and ran for a touchdown to tie the score. From that point on, the game belonged to the Dallas offense. The Cowboys went on to win 30–13. Smith rushed for 132 yards and two touchdowns and was named the MVP.

In 1995, the Cowboys played in their eighth Super Bowl. Their opponent was the Pittsburgh Steelers. The teams had faced each other twice in the 1970s for the championship, and Pittsburgh had won both times. The Cowboys wanted revenge.

Aikman, Smith, and Irvin led the way for the Dallas offense. However, the Cowboys were up by just three points in the fourth quarter. That's when Larry Brown made his second **interception** of the game and returned it for a touchdown. Dallas won 27–17 and celebrated its fifth NFL championship.

LEFT: Troy Aikman fires a pass against the Buffalo Bills.
ABOVE: Larry Brown heads for the end zone against the Pittsburgh Steelers.

Go-To Guys

To be a true star in the NFL, you need more than fast feet and a big body. You have to be a "go-to guy"—someone the coach wants on the field at the end of a big game. Cowboys fans have had a lot to cheer about over the years, including these great stars …

THE PIONEERS

DON PERKINS
DALLAS COWBOYS   FULLBACK

DON PERKINS   Running Back

- BORN: 3/4/1938   • PLAYED FOR TEAM: 1961 TO 1968

Don Perkins was small but very fast. He was the team's top running back in the 1960s. Perkins was voted to the Pro Bowl six times. When he retired, he was fourth on the NFL's all-time rushing list.

BOB LILLY   Defensive Lineman

- BORN: 7/26/1939   • PLAYED FOR TEAM: 1961 TO 1974

Bob Lilly was big, strong, and fast. Opposing teams never knew whether they should run their plays right at him or try to avoid him completely. It didn't matter because he always seemed to make the tackle. Lilly was voted **All-Pro** seven times.

MEL RENFRO Defensive Back

- BORN: 12/30/1941 • PLAYED FOR TEAM: 1964 TO 1977

Mel Renfro was a star at two positions, safety and cornerback. He also returned two kickoffs and a punt for touchdowns during his career. Renfro was chosen to play in the Pro Bowl in each of his first 10 NFL seasons.

ROGER STAUBACH Quarterback

- BORN: 2/5/1942 • PLAYED FOR TEAM: 1969 TO 1979

Roger "The Dodger" Staubach could win games with his arm or his legs. No matter the score, he never gave up. In all, Staubach led the team back from the edge of defeat to thrilling victories 23 times.

RANDY WHITE Defensive Lineman

- BORN: 1/15/1953 • PLAYED FOR TEAM: 1975 TO 1988

Randy White was nicknamed the "Manster" because someone once joked that he was half-man and half-monster. White had incredible quickness for a player his size. From 1978 to 1985, he was named All-Pro seven times.

TONY DORSETT Running Back

- BORN: 4/7/1954 • PLAYED FOR TEAM: 1977 TO 1987

Tony Dorsett had good speed and great balance. Instead of running, he seemed to glide down the field. In a 1983 game, he took a handoff in his own end zone and raced 99 yards for a touchdown.

LEFT: Don Perkins
RIGHT: Tony Dorsett

MICHAEL IRVIN · Receiver

- BORN: 3/5/1966 · PLAYED FOR TEAM: 1988 TO 1999

Michael Irvin was tall, fast, and fearless. For him, catching a pass and getting crushed by two or three tacklers was like a badge of honor. In 1995, he gained 100 or more receiving yards in 11 games in a row.

TROY AIKMAN · Quarterback

- BORN: 11/21/1966 · PLAYED FOR TEAM: 1989 TO 2000

Troy Aikman led the Cowboys to the Super Bowl three times in the 1990s. He was an accurate passer who loved to win. Aikman was always more interested in the final score than in his own statistics. He was voted into the Hall of Fame in 2006.

JAY NOVACEK · Tight End

- BORN: 10/24/1962 · PLAYED FOR TEAM: 1990 TO 1995

Jay Novacek was everything a team looks for in a tight end. He was big and fast, with soft hands and quick feet. No one was better at finding ways to get open, and few players worked harder on blocking.

EMMITT SMITH · Running Back

- BORN: 5/15/1969 · PLAYED FOR TEAM: 1990 TO 2002

At 5′ 9″, Emmitt Smith was small for an NFL running back, but no one ran with more heart or desire. Smith gained 1,000 or more yards 11 years in a row and topped the league in touchdowns three times. He retired as the league's all-time leading rusher.

LARRY ALLEN   Guard

• BORN: 11/27/1971   • PLAYED FOR TEAM: 1994 TO 2005

Larry Allen made a name for himself by flattening defensive players. Though he weighed more than 300 pounds, he was amazingly quick and *nimble*. Allen was voted to the Pro Bowl 10 times during his 12 seasons with the Cowboys.

TONY ROMO   Quarterback

• BORN: 4/21/1980   • FIRST YEAR WITH TEAM: 2004

Tony Romo waited more than two years before he got his chance to be the Dallas quarterback. In his first full season, he threw 36 touchdown passes and was named to the Pro Bowl. Romo led the Cowboys to the playoffs that year and again in 2009.

DeMARCUS WARE   Linebacker

• BORN: 7/31/1982   • FIRST YEAR WITH TEAM: 2005

When opposing quarterbacks scanned the Dallas defense, they always looked for DeMarcus Ware first. He was a dangerous pass-rusher who was almost impossible to block one-on-one. In 2008, Ware tied a record by **sacking** the passer 10 games in a row. He finished with 20 sacks that season.

ABOVE: Larry Allen

Calling the Shots

For their first 29 seasons, the Cowboys were led by Tom Landry. He had been a player and assistant coach in the NFL in the 1950s. As the leader of the Cowboys, he became one of the most famous coaches in football. Landry looked very *conservative* standing on the sidelines, but he wasn't afraid to try new ideas. One of his *innovations* was the "Flex Defense," which used three linebackers behind four linemen.

Landry was just as creative on offense. His players set up in a dozen or more different ways during a game to confuse opponents. Sometimes, Landry used two quarterbacks, switching them on each play. He also used the **shotgun snap** to protect his quarterback. Landry led the Cowboys to 21 **postseason** victories, including two Super Bowl championships.

The man who replaced Landry was Jimmy Johnson. Dallas was 1–15 in Johnson's first season, but three years later the team won another Super Bowl. He rebuilt the Cowboys through the draft with players such as Emmitt Smith, Russell Maryland, and

Jerry Jones and Jimmy Johnson share the Super Bowl trophy.

Darren Woodson. Each played a key role in the team's success. Johnson became famous for his trades on draft day. He made more than 50 in his five years with the Cowboys.

Thanks to Landry and Johnson, coaching the Cowboys is one of the most glamorous jobs in sports. Among those who followed these two legends were Barry Switzer, Bill Parcells, Wade Phillips, and Jason Garrett. Each of them worked for owner Jerry Jones. He bought the team in 1989. No one wanted to win more than Jones. He usually walked the sideline during Dallas games. When Jones was unhappy with a player or coach, he never hesitated to make his opinion heard.

One Great Day

The final game of the 1979 season for the Cowboys promised to be a good one. Dallas was hosting the Washington Redskins. Both teams were 10–5. The winner would claim the **NFC East** crown. Win or lose, it was a game everyone in Dallas wanted to see. Roger Staubach was nearing the end of his great career. At age 37, he was ready to retire.

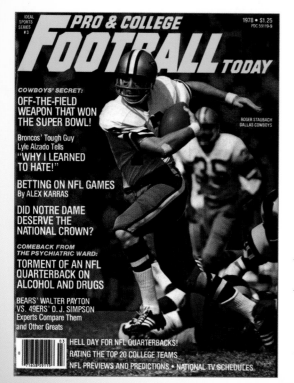

Things started badly for the Cowboys. The Redskins took a 17–0 lead and looked like they were in complete control. Staubach wouldn't go down without a fight. He rallied the Cowboys to three touchdowns, and they moved ahead

21–17. The Redskins came right back and went up 34–21.

Again, Staubach brought his team back. He closed the gap to 34–28 with a touchdown pass to Ron Springs, but time was running out. All Washington had to do was make a first down to run out the clock. On third down, they handed the ball to John Riggins. Larry Cole met him head-on and stopped the powerful runner in his tracks. The Redskins had to punt.

Staubach went to work. He guided Dallas to the 8-yard line with under a minute left. Dallas called a pass play. Staubach faded back and spotted Tony Hill angling for the end zone. He lofted a perfect pass, and Hill caught it for the game-tying score. Rafael Septien booted the extra point for a 35–34 victory.

"That was absolutely the most thrilling sixty minutes I ever spent on a football field," Staubach remembered years later. The fourth-quarter comeback win was the 23rd of his career—and his 14th in the final two minutes.

Legend Has It

Was Bob Hayes the fastest receiver ever in the NFL?

LEGEND HAS IT that he was. In fact, when he joined the Cowboys in 1965, Hayes was the world's fastest human. He was the first person to run the 60-yard dash in 6.0 seconds and the first to run the 100-yard dash in 9.1 seconds. Hayes won two gold medals in the 1964 *Summer Olympics*, and then led the NFL with 12 touchdowns the following year. He caught 371 passes and scored 76 touchdowns during his 11-year career.

ABOVE: Bob Hayes

Did the Cowboys have a "two-headed" quarterback?

LEGEND HAS IT that they did—twice! In 1963, coach Tom Landry had Eddie LeBaron and Don Meredith take turns on each down. One would jog to the sideline, while the other would join the huddle and call Landry's next play. In 1971, Landry did the same thing with Craig Morton and Roger Staubach. Teammates often had to look twice to make sure they knew which quarterback was in the game.

Which Cowboy had the greatest five minutes in football?

LEGEND HAS IT that Lee Roy Jordan did. Jordan was a swift, powerful linebacker who surprised opponents with his ability to cover pass receivers. No one was more surprised than quarterback Ken Anderson when the Cincinnati Bengals faced Dallas in 1973. In the first quarter of their game, Jordan stopped three Cincinnati drives in a row, ending each with an interception. Jordan ran one back for a 31-yard touchdown. In his 14 years with the Cowboys, Jordan intercepted 32 passes during the regular season and four more during the playoffs.

The Cowboys were one of the best teams in football in 1975. The same was true of the Minnesota Vikings. When they met in the playoffs that winter, everyone knew it would be a thrilling game.

The Cowboys had a great defense led by Harvey Martin, Cliff Harris, and Charlie Waters. Roger Staubach was in charge of the Dallas offense. Against Minnesota's "Purple People Eaters," he had to avoid hard-hitting defenders all day long. The outcome of the game was in doubt until the end of the fourth quarter. With time running out, the Vikings went on a long touchdown drive that gave them a 14–10 lead.

Staubach and the Cowboys got the ball back on their own 15-yard line with less than two minutes left. Dallas moved down the field, but the Minnesota defense stiffened. The Cowboys had time left for just one more play. Staubach told receiver Drew Pearson to sprint toward

DEFENSIVE END
HARVEY MARTIN

COWBOYS

the end zone. The Dallas quarterback would launch a long pass and "pray" for the best.

As the ball soared through the air, Pearson bumped one Viking defender, darted in front of another, caught the ball, and scored the winning touchdown. Minnesota fans were in shock, as the Cowboys celebrated their incredible victory. To this day, Dallas fans call Staubach's amazing pass the "Hail Mary" after a popular prayer.

LEFT: Harvey Martin   **ABOVE**: Drew Pearson shakes free after catching Roger Staubach's "Hail Mary" pass.

G ame day in Dallas is like no other in the NFL. The team's stadium offers so many fun things for fans to do. Some people don't even take a seat before kickoff. They stay in the Party Pass sections, where they can order all sorts of delicious food and watch the game on television.

Fans can also take an art tour at the stadium. This was the idea of Jerry Jones. He paid 18 artists to create paintings, sculptures, and original works that are displayed in and around the building.

Dallas is also home to football's most famous cheerleaders. In 1976, the Cowboys turned their cheerleading squad into a professional dance team. The Dallas Cowboys Cheerleaders soon became almost as famous as the players. After seeing how much the fans loved the cheerleaders, many NFL teams copied this idea.

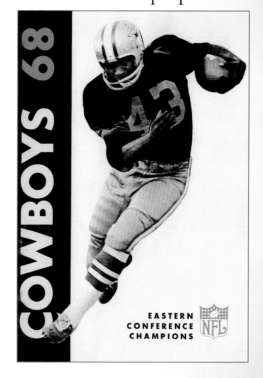

COWBOYS 68

EASTERN
CONFERENCE
CHAMPIONS NFL

LEFT: The Dallas Cowboys Cheerleaders
ABOVE: Fans bought this guide during the 1968 season.

Timeline

I n this timeline, each Super Bowl is listed under the year it was played. Remember that the Super Bowl is held early in the year and is actually part of the previous season. For example, Super Bowl XLVI was played on February 5, 2012, but it was the championship of the 2011 NFL season.

1965
Bob Hayes leads the NFL with 12 touchdown receptions.

1982
Danny White makes the Pro Bowl.

1960
The Cowboys join the NFL.

1972
The Cowboys win Super Bowl VI.

1978
Dallas wins its second championship.

Tex Schramm and Tom Landry are shown in 1960.

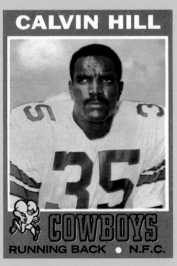

Calvin Hill starred in Super Bowl VI.

Emmitt Smith was the MVP of Super Bowl XXVIII.

Jason Witten

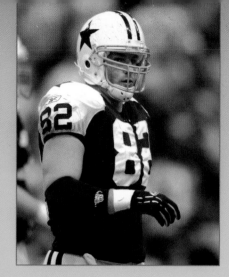

1993
The Cowboys win Super Bowl XXVII.

1994
The Cowboys win Super Bowl XXVIII.

2012
Jason Witten is voted to his eighth Pro Bowl.

1989
Jerry Jones buys the team.

1996
Dallas wins its fifth Super Bowl.

2011
DeMarcus Ware has 19.5 sacks.

Deion Sanders led the Dallas defense in the mid-1990s.

Fun Facts

THROW IT TO EMMITT!

Emmitt Smith was such a good runner with the Cowboys that fans *overlooked* his skill as a pass receiver. From 1991 to 1997, he caught

40 or more passes each season. When Jay Novacek and Michael Irvin were covered, Troy Aikman always knew he could find Emmitt!

DOUBLE DUTY

The Cowboys have had several stars who played more than one position. Danny White was the team's punter and quarterback during the 1980s. Deion Sanders lined up at defensive back and receiver in Super Bowl XXX.

THIS MEANS TROUBLE

In the 1960s and 1970s, the Cowboys were one of the scariest teams in football. Their defense was nicknamed the "Doomsday Defense."

ABOVE: Danny White
RIGHT: Herschel Walker

LET'S MAKE A DEAL

In 1989, the Cowboys and Minnesota Vikings made the NFL's biggest trade ever. A total of 18 players were swapped, including Dallas star Herschel Walker.

TEE TIME

Had Tony Romo not made it in the NFL, you might have seen him on the professional golf tour. Romo often plays alongside pros at charity tournaments. In 2012, he was in the same group as Phil Mickelson and Tiger Woods.

RUNNING THE NUMBERS

The Cowboys have always been football pioneers. Under Tom Landry, they became the first NFL team to use a computer to predict how young players would do once they joined the team.

SAY CHEESE

Someone who is often overlooked in the Cowboys' success is Gil Brandt. He worked for the team from 1960 to 1988 and found many of the players who became stars in Dallas. Before Brandt joined the Cowboys, he was a baby photographer.

Talking Football

"Troy was all about the team. He was for winning football games. He could have passed for big yards if he wanted, but he did what was best for the team."

▶ **Jerry Jones,** *on Troy Aikman*

"A winner never stops trying."

▶ **Tom Landry,** *on giving 100 percent no matter what the score*

"We knew what the rules were, and we knew we had to abide by them. You have to have some guidelines and you have to have some *discipline.*"

▶ **Roger Staubach,** *on playing for Tom Landry, who was known for being strict*

"You've got to look at the mistakes you made and see what you can do to eliminate them."

▶ **DeMarcus Ware,** *on how he tries to improve on the field*

"I don't think about any individual stats or any of that stuff. Any time you step on the field, you've got to have confidence in your abilities as a team."

▶ **Tony Romo,** *on being a team player*

"He was one tough individual. He played with many injuries and was very, very ***competitive***."

▶ **Lee Roy Jordan,** *on Don Meredith*

"This is a great thrill for me. It is special to me because now I can join the most ***exclusive*** group of players in football history."

▶ **Tony Dorsett,** *on being elected to the Hall of Fame*

LEFT: Jerry Jones   **ABOVE:** DeMarcus Ware

Great Debates

People who root for the Cowboys love to compare their favorite moments, teams, and players. Some debates have been going on for years! How would you settle these classic football arguments?

Troy Aikman was the Cowboys' top Super Bowl performer ...

... because he led Dallas to three championships in four years. Aikman (**LEFT**) was all about winning. In Super Bowl XXVII, Aikman was named MVP after throwing four touchdown passes against the Buffalo Bills. One year later, he led the team to another championship against the Bills, despite suffering from a *concussion*. In his third Super Bowl, Aikman tossed a scoring pass against the Pittsburgh Steelers.

Are you forgetting Chuck Howley? He was the team's top Super Bowl star ...

... because he was named the MVP in Super Bowl V—even though Dallas lost the game! Howley was all over the field that day, intercepting two passes and pouncing on a fumble. In Super Bowl VI, Howley was even better. His fumble recovery set up the first Dallas score. In the fourth quarter, he intercepted a pass that sealed the team's first championship.

... because they had amazing talent and great discipline. The championship teams of the 1970s were full of superstars. The offense featured Roger Staubach, Calvin Hill, Tony Dorsett, and Drew Pearson. Bob Lilly, Randy White, Harvey Martin, and Cliff Harris led the defense. These players took pride in avoiding mistakes and working together as one.

Jimmy Johnson's teams would take Landry's Cowboys apart ...

... because they were just too big, too fast, and too talented. It would be a long, painful day for the Doomsday Defense. Troy Aikman led a great offense that included Emmitt Smith, Daryl Johnston, Jay Novacek, and Michael Irvin. Under Johnson (RIGHT), the defense was fearless and lightning-quick. No doubt it would be a fun game to watch, but the Super Bowl teams of the early 1990s would just be too much for Landry's teams to handle.

For the Record

The great Cowboys teams and players have left their marks on the record books. These are the "best of the best" …

Chuck Howley

Randy White

COWBOYS AWARD WINNERS

WINNER	AWARD	YEAR
Tom Landry	Coach of the Year	1966
Calvin Hill	Rookie of the Year*	1969
Chuck Howley	Super Bowl V MVP	1971
Roger Staubach	Super Bowl VI MVP	1972
Tom Landry	Coach of the Year	1975
Tony Dorsett	Rookie of the Year	1977
Harvey Martin	Defensive Player of the Year	1977
Harvey Martin	Super Bowl XII co-MVP	1978
Randy White	Super Bowl XII co-MVP	1978
Emmitt Smith	Offensive Rookie of the Year	1990
Troy Aikman	Super Bowl XXVII MVP	1993
Emmitt Smith	Most Valuable Player	1993
Emmitt Smith	Super Bowl XXVIII MVP	1994
Larry Brown	Super Bowl XXX MVP	1996

* An award given to the league's best first-year player.

Fans bought this pennant during the team's early years.

COWBOYS ACHIEVEMENTS

ACHIEVEMENT	YEAR
NFC Champions	1970
NFC Champions	1971
Super Bowl VI Champions	1971*
NFC Champions	1975
NFC Champions	1977
Super Bowl XII Champions	1977*
NFC Champions	1978
NFC Champions	1992
Super Bowl XXVII Champions	1992*
NFC Champions	1993
Super Bowl XXVIII Champions	1993*
NFC Champions	1995
Super Bowl XXX Champions	1995*

* Super Bowls are played early the following year, but the game
is counted as the championship of this season.

WIDE RECEIVER
DREW PEARSON

ABOVE: Drew Pearson starred for the Cowboys in the 1970s.
LEFT: Deion Sanders makes a tackle. He caught a touchdown pass in Super Bowl XXX.

Pinpoints

The history of a football team is made up of many smaller stories. These stories take place all over the map—not just in the city a team calls "home." Match the pushpins on these maps to the **Team Facts**, and you will begin to see the story of the Cowboys unfold!

TEAM FACTS

1 Dallas, Texas—*The Cowboys have played in this area since 1960.*

2 West Covina, California—*Troy Aikman was born here.*

3 Mission, Texas—*Tom Landry was born here.*

4 New Orleans, Louisiana—*The Cowboys won their first Super Bowl here.*

5 Cincinnati, Ohio—*Roger Staubach was born here.*

6 Pensacola, Florida—*Emmitt Smith was born here.*

7 Baltimore, Maryland—*Calvin Hill was born here.*

8 South River, New Jersey—*Drew Pearson was born here.*

9 Rochester, Pennsylvania—*Tony Dorsett was born here.*

10 Phoenix, Arizona—*Darren Woodson was born here.*

11 Mexico City, Mexico—*Rafael Septien was born here.*

12 Tokyo, Japan—*The Cowboys played in the 2000 American Bowl* here.*

* The American Bowl was the annual NFL game played outside the United States from 1986 to 2005.

Darren Woodson

Glossary

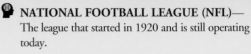
ALL-PRO—An honor given to the best players at their positions at the end of each season.

AMERICAN FOOTBALL LEAGUE (AFL)—The football league that began play in 1960 and later merged with the NFL.

COMPETITIVE—Having a strong desire to win.

CONCUSSION—A head injury that affects the brain.

CONSERVATIVE—Unwilling to take risks.

DECADE—A period of 10 years; also specific periods, such as the 1950s.

DISCIPLINE—Behavior that follows rules.

DOMINATE—Completely control through the use of power.

DRAFT—The annual meeting during which teams choose from a group of the best college players.

EXCLUSIVE—Small and special.

FUMBLE—A ball that is dropped by the player carrying it.

HALL OF FAME—A museum where great players are honored. Pro football has its own Hall of Fame.

INNOVATIONS—New ideas.

INTERCEPTION—A pass that is caught by the defensive team.

LOGO—A symbol or design that represents a company or team.

MOST VALUABLE PLAYER (MVP)—The award given each year to the league's best player; also given to the best player in the Super Bowl and Pro Bowl.

NATIONAL FOOTBALL CONFERENCE (NFC)—One of two groups of teams that make up the NFL.

NATIONAL FOOTBALL LEAGUE (NFL)—The league that started in 1920 and is still operating today.

NFC EAST—A division for teams that play in the eastern part of the country.

NFL CHAMPIONSHIP GAME—The game played to decide the winner of the league each year from 1933 to 1969.

NIMBLE—Quick and light in movement or action.

OVERLOOKED—Ignored or not noticed.

PLAYOFFS—The games played after the regular season to determine which teams play in the Super Bowl.

POSTSEASON—Another term for playoffs.

PRO BOWL—The NFL's all-star game, played after the regular season.

PROFESSIONAL—Paid to play.

RETRACTABLE—Able to be pulled back.

RIVALRY—Extremely emotional competition.

SACKING—Tackling the quarterback behind the line of scrimmage.

SHOTGUN SNAP—A formation in which the quarterback lines up two or three steps behind the center.

SUMMER OLYMPICS—An international sports competition held every four years.

SUPER BOWL—The championship of the NFL, played between the winners of the National Football Conference and American Football Conference.

TRADITION—A belief or custom that is handed down from generation to generation.

OVERTIME

TEAM SPIRIT introduces a great way to stay up to date with your team! Visit our **OVERTIME** link and get connected to the latest and greatest updates. **OVERTIME** serves as a young reader's ticket to an exclusive web page—with more stories, fun facts, team records, and photos of the Cowboys. Content is updated during and after each season. The **OVERTIME** feature also enables readers to send comments and letters to the author! Log onto:

www.norwoodhousepress.com/library.aspx

and click on the tab: **TEAM SPIRIT** to access **OVERTIME**.

Read all the books in the series to learn more about professional sports. For a complete listing of the baseball, basketball, football, and hockey teams in the **TEAM SPIRIT** series, visit our website at:

www.norwoodhousepress.com/library.aspx

On the Road

DALLAS COWBOYS
1 Legends Way
Arlington, Texas 76011
972-556-9900
www.dallascowboys.com

THE PRO FOOTBALL HALL OF FAME
2121 George Halas Drive NW
Canton, Ohio 44708
330-456-8207
www.profootballhof.com

On the Bookshelf

To learn more about the sport of football, look for these books at your library or bookstore:

- Frederick, Shane. *The Best of Everything Football Book.* North Mankato, Minnesota: Capstone Press, 2011.

- Jacobs, Greg. *The Everything Kids' Football Book: The All-Time Greats, Legendary Teams, Today's Superstars—And Tips on Playing Like a Pro.* Avon, Massachusetts: Adams Media Corporation, 2010.

- Editors of *Sports Illustrated for Kids. 1st and 10: Top 10 Lists of Everything in Football.* New York, New York: Sports Illustrated Books, 2011.

47

Index

About the Author

MARK STEWART has written more than 50 books on football and over 150 sports books for kids. He grew up in New York City during the 1960s rooting for the Giants and Jets, and was lucky enough to meet players from both teams. Mark comes from a family of writers. His grandfather was Sunday Editor of *The New York Times,* and his mother was Articles Editor of *Ladies' Home Journal* and *McCall's.* Mark has profiled hundreds of athletes over the past 25 years. He has also written several books about his native New York and New Jersey, his home today. Mark is a graduate of Duke University, with a degree in history. He lives and works in a home overlooking Sandy Hook, New Jersey. You can contact Mark through the Norwood House Press website.

mL

9-15